Whispers

From The

Heart

Larry L. Black

Contents

If I Promise

If I promise it won't mean too much.
would you chase my tears away?
Just need a quiet, soothing touch,
to make it through the day.
If I promise not to get too close,
could I put my trust in you?
Just need to know you'll keep it safe,
and above all keep it true.
Can I have a corner of your heart,
that I could keep as mine?
A place I know belongs to me,
at least for just this time.
If I promise not to stay too long,
would you hold me close and tight?
Just need to feel the warmth of you,
on this dark and lonely night.
I promise it won't mean too much,
I promise not to care.
Just need to know I'm not alone,
that someone else is there.

Elusive Friends of the Heart

Sometimes friendship has a
way of tripping over itself.
Each of us searching for
the comfort of a friend,
yet afraid to give too much,
or to turn the pages of the
book within our hearts that
will reveal the pain within.
Each of us reaching out
with hopes of finding that
special person to share the
secrets of the heart.
Yet once found,
too afraid that secrets
shared will become the
poison that makes a
friendship die.

Each of us wanting to wrap
ourselves in the warm blanket
of each other's strength,
but fearful that the warmth
will become too suffocating.
Too afraid to enjoy the
true warmth of friendship's
fire.
Yes, sometimes friendship
has a way of tripping over itself.
Or perhaps it is each of us.
Tripping over the fear
within our hearts.

For Just a Little While

The night closes around us,
comforting with its shadows of
gray and silver moon.
I sit in the quiet nearness of you
ever aware of beating hearts, and words
unsaid drifting like
crystal feathers in the air.
I close my eyes and wonder.
Wonder, could you hold me once again?
Hold me please, for just a little while?
And, it's okay to pretend… to
pretend that you love me.
You can think of days gone by
and forget the time that we call now.
I wonder. Could you hold me
for just a little while? Hold me so I
can forget the nights that tears
were the sheep I counted to
a sleep without you.

So I can forget the empty days spent
in dreams of loving you, can forget the loneliness
of a life without the nearness of you.
As the night closes around us,
it's okay to pretend you care.
No.
Don't open your eyes and see the reality of you and me.
Please, just pretend. Forget the time
that we call now.
I wonder, if you do these things
could you hold me?
Hold me… for just a little while.

For Peace and Love

I take a look at life and see,
so many wondrous things.
The stars, the moon, and butterflies
that fly with golden wings.
I see the wondrous light of dawn,
the flight of a graceful dove.
The beauty of a wild rose,
the clouds that drift above.
I see a happy child at play,
a ball goes bouncing high.
The saddened face of a crippled child,
as he reaches for the sky.
I see a war with many deaths,
the murder of a land.
The victor with a smiling face,
a pride that's not so grand.
I see a troubled land of love,
and foolish talks of peace.
A land that wants so many things,
yet guns that never cease.
I take a look at life and see
the clouds that drift above,
The saddened face of a crippled child,
who hopes for peace and love.

Fragile Hearts and Gossamer Wings

I once thought that a heart
full of love was a forever thing.
Now I know it's like fragile
rose petals that have been
scattered in the wind…leaving
just a scent of once was.
I used to think that dreams
were full of what could be, rich
with hope for brighter tomorrows.
In fact, they are like gossamer
wings fluttering out of control.
Unstable and without direction.
There was a time I thought passion
was beautiful and precious, the one
ingredient required for lasting love.
Funny how it turned out to be double
edged, tainted with the desire for the
mysteries of the unknown.
I once knew that love would be forever
in my heart. That I would be loved with
uncompromising innocence and trust.

It seems that love is simply the direction
of the heart, the momentum gained
when innocence is lost.
Fragile hearts and gossamer wings. The
things that love are made of. Double edged
passions and innocence lost. The things that
break a heart. I once thought I knew
of these things...but perhaps they are
just a scent of once was.

Fuzzy Color of Broken Dreams

Sorting through
pieces of broken dreams,
trying to find the memory
of you.
Holding pieces of dreams
in my mind's eye, trying to
remember the shape of
our love…
Trying to fit the pieces
back together again.
It's funny how broken
dreams don't just fade
away quietly in the night.
They invade your very heart,
turning into tortured whispers
of what could have been,
seeping…into the shadows
of your mind.
Memories just out of reach,
unclear with the fuzzy
color that broken
dreams become.

Hard to remember what
the dreams once held.
Sorting through them,
trying to find the
memory of our love…

Angel Mine

I felt an angel near today,
though one I couldn't see.
I felt an angel oh-so-close,
sent to comfort me.
I felt an angel's gentle kiss,
soft upon my cheek.
And oh, without a single word,
of caring it did speak.
I felt an angel's loving touch,
soft upon my heart.
And with that touch I felt the pain,
and hurt within depart.
I felt an angel's tepid tears,
fall softly next to mine.
And knew that as those tears did dry,
a new day would be mine.
I felt an angel's silken wings,
enfold me with pure love.
And felt a strength within me grow,
a strength sent from above.
I felt an angel oh-so-close,
though one I couldn't see.
I felt an angel near today,
sent to comfort me.

Lipstick Kiss

So this is it, you've had your say
you're walking out the door,
You've found another man to love,
don't want me anymore.
Before you leave, just one request,
so I can make it through the night.
Leave a lipstick kiss on the mirror,
as a token of love once right.
Leave a lipstick kiss on the mirror,
and when I look at it each day,
I'll remember the loved we shared
before you took it all away.
I'll remember how you used to smile,
when I told you I loved you.
I'll remember how you promised,
that our love was strong and true.
Leave a lipstick kiss on the mirror, please,
so when I wipe the tears from my eyes,
I'll know you loved me for a little while,
that your words of love weren't lies.

Above all darling, I'll think of you,
when I'm alone and wondering why,
my love just wasn't good enough,
why it ended in good-bye.
Leave a lipstick kiss on the mirror,
then please, please walk away.
I'll always remember the love we shared,
before you took it all away.

Melody of the Heart

Lost within the shadow
dance of candlelight,
my mind keeps rhythm
with the flame.
Thoughts flicker to moments
once tender, passions
once shared.
Happiness once mine.
I taste my tears soft against
my lips and am reminded
of how fragile
a man can be.
How tender the heart.
Each tear strikes a
chord within me,
a song played gently
upon my soul.
A melody that whispers
of lost dreams
and the consequence
of innocence.

Funny how a melody
composed of the
heart can make a
man so weak,
Can leave him lost.
Lost within the
shadow dance of
candlelight and tears.

Memories of Love

The quiet of the night embraces me as if
encountering an old friend, and
I settle into the comfort of that which I know.
Sheltered by my familiar cocoon of loneliness,
I am tormented by desires dormant
yet not forgotten.
My eyes remember the loveliness of flesh,
exposed in subtle and sexy ways.
My arms remember the feel of an embrace,
tight with need and desire,
My lips remember the sweetness of a loving kiss,
the warmth of breath expelled in ecstasy.
My tongue remembers the taste of love,
sweet and poignant at the moment of release.
My body remembers the closeness of another,
warm and receptive to the touch of love.
I stay quiet in my cocoon of loneliness,
discontent with the comfort of memories.
Needing the warmth of human touch,
the strength of a hand to hold.
I settle into the comfort of that
which I know, embraced by
the quiet of the night.

Reflections at Dawn

I watch the sun peek over the horizon,
winking its early morning hello as if cautious
of the new day.
The clouds, full of brazen beauty,
stretch lazily across the horizon, beckoning
with their softness.
It's at quiet times such as this that I think of love lost.
Of broken dreams and promises.
Could it be that love is like the sun? Fierce and
unrelenting at one moment, and hiding
in the clouds the next…
almost like a game of hide and seek – reduced to
nothing but a countdown and meaningless chance.
When the game is over, surely the only
victor is pain.
Pain not of the limb or muscle that can be eased
with care and attention. No,
it is a pain within the very soul.
Pain that strips away the very things
that makes one whole.
The trust, the caring, and above all – need
by another human being.

I sit, stripped of these things, and watch the sun
stretch higher into the sky. I watch the clouds
knowing that, like them, a
part of me has drifted away.
I tuck away the pain… unsure of what the day will bring.
Hoping. Hoping with all of my heart
for a brighter tomorrow.

Take the Time

Take the time today
to see the beauty of your life.
Take the time to let
the innocence of a child touch your heart,
the laughter of a friend brighten your day,
the warmth of a touch make you smile.
Take the time…
Take the time today
to acknowledge the love that surrounds you.
Take the time to cherish
the joy that friendship brings to your heart,
the strength that family brings to your soul,
the peace that love brings to your life.
Take the time…
before time slips away.
Take the time today
to become your own best friend.
Take the time to know
that you will never be perfect, but will be loved anyway.
That you have imperfections that make you unique,
that it's okay to like yourself
just the way you are.

Take the time…
Take the time today
to experience the joy that life brings.
Take the time to recognize
that living is more than just doing, it is feeling.
That the joy in living comes from the joy within your heart,
that you are the key to your own happiness.
Take the time…
before time slips away.

The Mask

I want to
take off my mask,
just once…and
set my emotions free.
For a single day I want
to lose all identity.
Then, when I am stripped
of myself, take my hand.
Gently, let me know of love.
When I am cold,
cover me with your warmth.
Touch me with your soul.
When I am warm,
cool me with your touch.
Be my torch to light
the way.
Be my world.
Completely,
totally
honestly.
Let me laugh until I cry,
cry until I can cry no longer.

Be my friend,

my lover,

my life.

Show me love as

if I had never seen it before.

And then,

I will put myself back on.

Replace the mask.

Continue the masquerade.

And someday, see you again.

This Place Called Now

In this place called now, I am alone.
Afraid of the me I've come to be.
Afraid of the loneliness.
This place. Full of doubts and fears.
Full of ghosts and shadows and friends,
and not having the strength to know
what face each might wear.
In this place, I wonder where dreams
go when they die... wonder if I ever
had dreams at all.
This place.
Rich with thoughts and the
beauty of what could have been.
This place.
Filled with confusion in wondering what will be.
In this place, I search for a hand
to hold. A hand to keep me
steady through the storm that
rages in my heart.
A hand to help me through the night.
In this place called now.
This place.
I am alone.
Afraid of the me
I've come to be.

Tick Tock of the Heart

My heart grows weary with
the ticking of the clock.
I exist in places of memories,
thoughts of tomorrow clouded
by the truths of today.
I seek not the burden of love
for it has shown itself to be
an enemy of my heart.
I trust not the strength in
friendship, for in its comfortable
weave is the thread of sorrow.
Each day becomes a highway to
the avenue of the night, an
intersection of lonely moments
and dangerous solitude.
I long for restful sleep to still the
echoes of my sighs. Peace from
the confusion of the soul.
Freedom from a heart that
needs too much.
Weary in
keeping time with the ticking
of the clock.

Truths

Night falls, and the darkness presses
against my heart with a soft persistence as
if trying to gain entry to my soul.
I sit by myself,
inside myself,
quietly nibbling at the crust of memories
called yesterday, while sipping
from the cup of reality called today.
Thoughts come and go.
The good and the bad
turned inside out.
Thoughts colored with the unmistakable
hue of sadness found most often in
the eyes of lost children and
of the old.
The night is quiet and
I am afraid
of the truths that the darkness holds.
Truths that have come too late
to a childish heart, that have come too
suddenly to an unsuspecting soul.
These truths are too simple to matter.
Too complex to ignore.

The truth that I have loved too deeply.

That I have trusted too much.

Have cried too often.

Believed too much in others

and not enough in myself.

Truths that leave me alone in the dark.

I sit by myself.

Inside myself.

Hoping to find the strength

to begin again,

with a strength I can call my own.

When a Single Teardrop Falls

Kisses gone but not forgotten
clinging to my lips like the
aftertaste of a sweet and heady wine.
Moments lost in the total rapture of
you. This is what I recall, when a single
teardrop falls.
When a single teardrop falls...
I remember laughter dancing on the
wind. You and I as one, sharing a
passion too strong for one heart.
Too new for doubt.
I smell the sweetness of our bodies
joined by a lust so pure that it
could take our breath away.
The result of a single caress...
a look...
a sigh...
I see us exploring our world with
faith and trust.

With love and sympathy.

With total abandon.

With childish glee.

This is what I recall.

When a

single

teardrop

falls.

You Forgot to Say Goodbye

I look back and realize that
in your heart, you left me long ago.
It's funny, but what causes the most pain
is knowing…
that you forgot to say goodbye.
The pain doesn't come from knowing that our
dreams, once exciting and new, are now just mine
alone. Or that love, once burning with the heat of
what could be, is now reduced to ashes of cold memories.
Doesn't come from the realization that you stopped
seeing that I needed the warmth that comes from holding
you. That you stopped seeing that I needed to be held.
It comes in knowing…
that you forgot to say goodbye.
It's not the times you forgot to see the tears caused
by the hurt of losing you or the way you neglected to see
the loneliness in my eyes. Not the way you forgot to see
the little boy in me, needing the comforting touch of you.
Doesn't come from the pain you caused in pushing
me away for the attention of another. Not the way you
stopped being the world I knew.
It comes in knowing…
that you forgot to say goodbye.
Wish I could stop the pain in knowing…
that you forgot to say goodbye.

About the Author

Larry L. Black, a cancer survivor, is an American poet and artist who currently resides in Durham, North Carolina. He served with honor in the U.S. military and has worked for the federal government in Germany, North Carolina, Virginia, Washington, D.C., and Florida.